3/02

24.⁰⁰

# The Hudson River

# The Hudson River

By Melissa Whitcraft

**Franklin Watts**
A Division of Grolier Publishing
New York • London • Hong Kong • Sydney
Danbury, Connecticut

*To SKW and ETW*
*With thanks for introducing me to*
*The Wild Hudson*

**Note to readers:** Definitions for words in **bold** can be found in the Glossary at the back of this book.

Photographs ©: Art Resource, NY: 34 (National Museum of American Art, Washington, D.C.), 42 (The Newark Museum); Betsy Imershein: 33, 37, 43 top, 51 bottom; Corbis-Bettmann: 36; Courtesy of The Adirondack Museum: 17, 18, 19, 21; Dean Color: cover, 8, 14, 22, 24, 25 left; Gamma-Liaison, Inc.: 5 top, 52 (S. Dooley), 12 (Hulton Getty); National Geographic Image Collection: 5 bottom, 30, 31, 35, 43 bottom (Melissa Farlow); North Wind Picture Archives: 11, 25 right; Photo Researchers: 53 (Georg Gerster), 49 top (Leonard Lee Rue III); The Image Works: 38 (Mulvehill), 45 (Lee Snider), 46, 49 bottom (Ted Spiegel), 50, 51 top (Perry Alan Werner); Tony Stone Images: 9 (E.R.I.M.), 28, 41 (Jake Rajs), 2 (A & L Sinibaldi).

Map by Bob Italiano.

Visit Franklin Watts on the Internet at:
http://publishing.grolier.com

**Library of Congress Cataloging-in-Publication Data**

Whitcraft, Melissa
    The Hudson River / by Melissa Whitcraft.
        p.      cm.— (Watts library)
    Includes bibliographical references and index.
    Summary: Take a journey along the Hudson River from its source in the mountains to its final destination in the Atlantic. Along the way, learn about the history of the river, interesting facts about river towns, and how the Hudson has affected the history of the United States.
    ISBN 0-531-11739-1 (lib. bdg.)      0-531-16425-X (pbk.)
    1. Hudson River (NY and New Jersey) Description and travel—Juvenile literature. 2. Hudson River (NY and New Jersey)—History—Juvenile literature. 3. Hudson River Valley (NY and New Jersey)—History. Local Juvenile literature. [1. Hudson River (NY and New Jersey)] I. Title. II. Series.
F127.H5 1999
974.7'3—dc21                                                                99-28585
                                                                                  CIP

# Contents

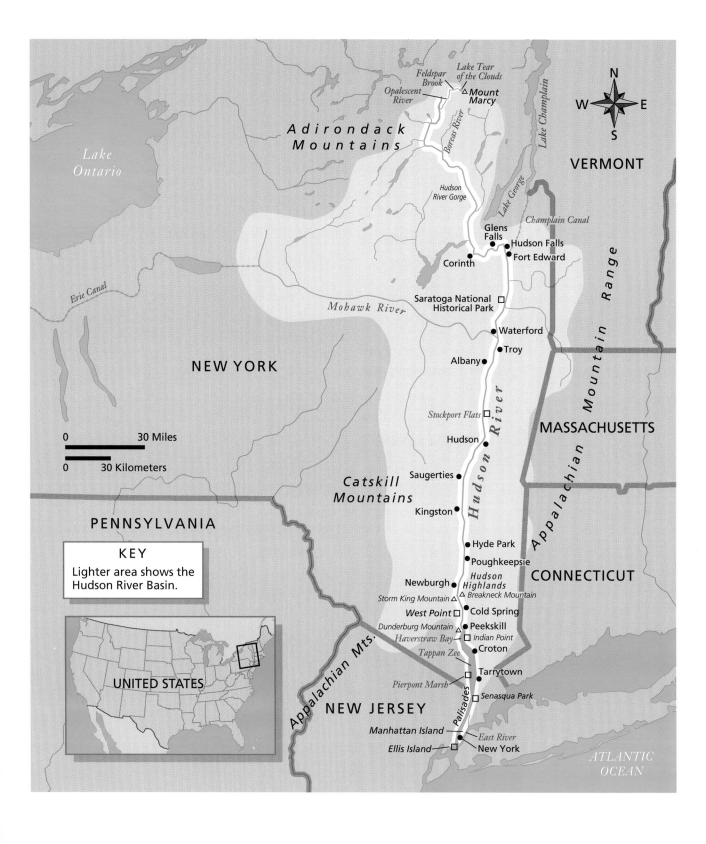

N
W    E
S

*Feldspar Brook*
*Lake Tear of the Clouds*
*Opalescent River*
△ Mount Marcy

**Adirondack Mountains**

*Boreas River*

*Lake Champlain*

VERMONT

*Lake Ontario*

*Hudson River Gorge*

*Lake George*

*Champlain Canal*

Glens Falls
● Hudson Falls
● Fort Edward
● Corinth

*Erie Canal*

*Mohawk River*

NEW YORK

□ Saratoga National Historical Park

● Waterford
● Troy
● Albany

*Appalachian Mountain Range*

MASSACHUSETTS

□ Stockport Flats

*Hudson River*

● Hudson

**Catskill Mountains**

● Saugerties

● Kingston

PENNSYLVANIA

**KEY**
Lighter area shows the
Hudson River Basin.

● Hyde Park
● Poughkeepsie

*Hudson Highlands*

Newburgh ●

CONNECTICUT

*Storm King Mountain* △ ▲ *Breakneck Mountain*

*West Point* □ ● Cold Spring

*Dunderburg Mountain* △ ● Peekskill

*Haverstraw Bay* □ *Indian Point*

*Tappan Zee* ● Croton

*Appalachian Mts.*

□ Tarrytown

*Pierpont Marsh*

□ Senasqua Park

*Palisades*

UNITED STATES

**NEW JERSEY**

*Manhattan Island* *East River*

*Ellis Island* □ ● New York

ATLANTIC OCEAN

0     30 Miles
0     30 Kilometers

# Chapter One

# The Hudson: A River of Opposites

High on Mount Marcy in the Adirondack State Park, a doe dips her head to drink the clear, swift water that rushes past her. Her fawn moves out of forest shadows and also drinks from the stream. This wilderness spot marks the headwaters of the remarkable Hudson, a river of trees, a river of cities.

Almost all of the 13,370 square miles

*Opposite: A satellite view shows New York and the surrounding districts. The view shows the mouth of the Hudson River and the Narrows.*

*An aerial view of the Adirondack Mountains*

(34,630 square kilometers) drained by the Hudson and its tributaries are in the state of New York. Trees cover sixty percent of the state, although most of its agricultural wealth centers on dairy farming. However, ninety percent of the state's 18,137,000 people (1997 estimate) live near urban areas. The largest city is New York City, one of the most heavily populated and commercially developed metropolises in the world.

The Hudson begins its journey to New York City by twisting through mountains formed fifteen million years ago and

continuing through rolling farmland. When the river reaches the city of Troy, it has traveled approximately 165 miles (265.5 km) and dropped 4,291 feet (1,308 meters). From Troy, which is only 2 feet (61 centimeters) above sea level, the river flows an additional 150 miles (241 km) to the Atlantic. This part of the Hudson is dramatically different from the narrower section north of Troy. It is now a spectacular tidal river, the largest freshwater **estuary** in the world.

## How the Hudson Was Formed

When the 3,000-foot-thick (914-m) glaciers covered North America ten thousand to twelve thousand

years ago, they deepened the Hudson's estuary bed and carved steep cliffs into its banks. When the glaciers retreated, they left behind large deposits of rock and other debris at the river's mouth. Called the Narrows and situated between Long Island and Staten Island, this ridge of ancient hills is a geological gateway. The Narrows lets Atlantic tides flow up and down the Hudson but protects the estuary from the full force of the ocean's currents.

# The First Settlers

Because the Hudson's harbor is so protected, people have always settled along the shores of the estuary. The first settlers were descendants of people from northeast Asia who crossed into northwestern North America over the **Bering Land Bridge** during the Ice Age. Eventually, the Woodland tribes, who inhabited the Hudson Valley beginning around 1500 B.C.E., replaced these people. Over the next three thousand years, migrants lived, farmed, and fished along the lower river. From the Manhattan tribes at the mouth of the river to the

*Opposite: Henry Hudson descending the Hudson River*

10

*Henry Hudson was the English navigator who discovered Hudson Bay and after whom the Hudson River is named.*

Mohicans near Troy, the aboriginal people understood the important connection between the river and its tides. Early Algonquins called the Hudson *Muhheakantuck*, which meant "the river that flows both ways."

When Henry Hudson, the English navigator and explorer, sailed his 84-foot (26-m) ship, the *Half Moon*, up Muhheakantuck on September 11, 1609, he thought he had found the much sought-after Northwest Passage. Europeans had been exploring the northeast coast of North America for over eighty years, hoping to find the legendary water route that would link Europe with Asia. Hudson knew that if this long, wide expanse of water were that particular route, his employer, the Dutch East India Company, would reward him greatly.

Just past what is now Albany, the river narrowed and became too shallow for Hudson's ship. Hudson thought he had failed. He didn't realize that the estuary he had explored was only part of an immensely fascinating river that would play an extremely important role in the development of this new continent. As we journey down this river that now bears the explorer's name, we will learn just how important the Hudson was then—and is today.

*The Hudson River begins at Lake Tear of the Clouds, high on Mount Marcy.*

# Chapter Two

# The Wild Hudson

In the summer of 1872, Verplanck Colvin set out to climb Mount Marcy, the highest mountain in the Adirondack State Park. Mount Marcy rises 5,344 feet (1,629 m) above sea level. When Colvin, a naturalist and a **surveyor** for the state of New York, reached 4,293 feet (1,308.5 m), he came upon a small glacial lake only 500 feet (152 m) long and 5 feet (1.5 m) deep. Realizing he had found the source of the Hudson River, he wrote that the "Summit water

15

(was) a minute, unpretending tear of the clouds. . . a lovely pool, shivering in the breezes of the mountains."

## The Source of the Hudson

The Hudson's source was later named Lake Tear of the Clouds. Because native Americans called Mount Marcy *Tahawus*, or "cloud splitter," Colvin's name was appropriate. Today, Lake Tear of the Clouds is still a bright mountain pool, surrounded by wind-bent trees of hemlock, balsam, and spruce. It remains a quiet, idyllic spot well worth the grueling 9-mile (14.5-km) climb to get there.

When the Hudson leaves Lake Tear of the Clouds and heads down through the mountains, it picks up two tributaries that add to its headwaters. One is the Feldspar Brook that flows in from the west over moss-covered rocks and narrow gorges. The other is the Opalescent River. Here, a mile below the rarified air of Mount Marcy, oaks and maples grow alongside taller evergreens, and the forest is thick with birds and woodland animals.

## Mining in the Adirondacks

In the nineteenth century, two developments changed the Adirondack Hudson forever. The first event was the discovery of iron in the mid 1800s. Soon, mining companies spread throughout the central Adirondacks, and the region was dotted with settlements, roads, blast furnaces, and **forges.** One

mining company, the MacIntyre Mine, burned more than an acre of trees a day in its furnaces to melt the iron ore.

*A nineteenth-century garnet mine on the North River*

Despite its initial success, however, the MacIntyre Mine closed in 1856. By the early 1900s, most other companies had shut down as well. Iron was mined again briefly during World War II in the 1940s, but ultimately the Adirondacks proved too inaccessible, and its ore too impure to make iron mining profitable.

None of the companies could have functioned at all, however, without the waterpower supplied by the region's rivers.

## Old Mining Towns

Adirondack mining companies created entire towns for their workers. The companies owned everything in these towns, from the products for sale in the company stores to the houses the miners lived in. Today, the mining settlements, which often included churches, band shells, and even tennis courts, are deserted ghost towns reclaimed by the forest forever.

Because of its location near Mount Marcy, the MacIntyre Mine relied heavily on the Hudson. Workers dammed the river and built waterwheels to power the giant sledgehammers of the forges.

# Logging Rules the River

The second event to change the Hudson was the advent of logging companies. The tall trees of the forest represented a fortune for lumber companies, and the river was the best way

to get the cut timber out of the mountains to the sawmills below. When the weather warmed in the spring, the logs were floated downriver in water swollen with melted snow and ice.

It was a dangerous trip for the log drivers who rode the rolling logs, particularly when they reached the Hudson River Gorge. At that point, high cliffs and fast rapids surrounded the river, and it dropped 220 feet (67 m) in 15 miles (24 km). The drivers had to maneuver their logs through these treacherous rapids without slipping to their death in the icy water that swirled around them.

*These log drivers are herding logs on the river. Notice how bare the landscape is where the log drivers have cut down the logs.*

After the drivers got the timber safely through the Gorge and past the Boreas River, the rest of the trip was easier. At Glens Falls, before the logs were processed at sawmills, they were contained behind the Big Boom to keep them from flowing downriver. The Big Boom, which was first used in 1851, was a structure made of huge timber rafts connected by metal chains. Sometimes the boom held so many logs that timber was backed up the river for 2 to 3 miles (3 to 4 km).

## Preserving the Adirondacks

Today, mostly due to the early efforts of surveyor Verplanck Colvin, the amount of lumber taken from the Adirondacks is controlled. Colvin spent twenty-eight years mapping the wilderness and realized that if it were destroyed, the entire Hudson River **watershed** would be in danger. Because the forests prevented soil erosion, kept moisture in the ground, and protected the river water from evaporating, the Hudson would dry up without them. Consequently, there would be no water for cities and **canals** downriver. Colvin's solution was to make the Adirondack wilderness a state park "to protect the sources of the Hudson" and to conserve the land for "healthful recreation."

The Albany drought in 1885 persuaded the state legislature of New York to follow through on Colvin's suggestions. Initially, New York set aside 2.6 million acres (1.05 million hectare) as the Adirondack Forest Preserve. The law stated that the trees in this preserve would never be cut down.

By 1892, Colvin had convinced New York to add approximately 3.4 million more acres (1.37 million ha) to the park. The additional land further protected the Hudson but also allowed responsible logging to take place within its borders. In 1894, a final Article XIV was added to insure that the initial forest preserve be "forever kept as wild forest lands."

*Verplank Colvin (top left) points out something in the distance to his team of surveyors on Mount Hurricane.*

*The hydroelectric dam ten miles from Glens Falls*

# Chapter Three

# The Harnessed Hudson

Outside the Adirondack Park, the Hudson drops through a narrow gorge where it meets the Sacandago River. Now, for the first time, motor boats appear on the water. The door to the wilderness has shut, and we are on a Hudson that has been transformed by the industrial and commercial needs of humankind.

*A feeder canal at Glens Falls*

## Using Dams Across the Hudson

The change is obvious almost immediately. Between the mill town of Corinth and the larger community of Glens Falls, five major dams cross the Hudson. Eliminating all natural rapids, the first two dams harness the river for a paper-processing company. The two dams belong to the Niagara-Mohawk Power Company, which produces electricity for the Hudson River Valley.

## Battle at Saratoga

Halfway between Fort Edward and Waterford, the Hudson passes Saratoga National Historical Park. At Saratoga, the Colonists won an important battle against the British during the Revolution. Under Major General Horatio Gates and with help from local farmers, the American army surrounded the British until they surrendered on October 17, 1777. The victory gave the Americans control of the upper Hudson River, stopped the British army in the north from uniting with its troops to the south, and encouraged the French to join the American side.

The fifth dam, which lies just above Glens Falls, is the Feeder Dam. It channels water from the river to the Feeder Canal. Built in the nineteenth century, the Feeder Canal runs parallel to the river until the Hudson turns south. At that point, the Feeder Canal continues east until it hooks up with the Champlain Canal. The Feeder Canal "feeds" the Champlain Canal with enough water from the Hudson to ensure that the canal can run its two highest **locks.**

Beyond Glens Falls, the Hudson flows down into Fort Edward where it meets the Champlain Canal. For the next 40 miles (64 km), the river and the canal flow as one through four more dams and seven locks. Today, these locks carry pleasure boats back and forth from Lake Champlain.

In the 1800s, however, this stretch of the Hudson served as a vibrant commercial waterway, and many of the towns along its banks flourished as industrial centers. Fort Edward was one such town. A century ago, it was famous for its huge blast furnaces that processed iron ore from the Adirondacks. Now this small town is famous again, unfortunately for a very disturbing reason.

## PCBs Pollute the River

The problem began in 1946 with the General Electric Company's plants in Hudson Falls and Fort Edward. The plants manufactured electric storage containers that used chemical compounds called PCBs as liquid insulation.

We now know that PCBs, or polychlorinated biphenyls, cause liver damage, cancer, brain dysfunction, and birth defects in humans. PCBs also destroy the **ecology** of natural environments. Because of their extreme **toxicity**, they were banned from use in the late 1970s. However, by then, the damage to the Hudson was done.

The PCBs have washed as far south as Manhattan, but most of the Hudson's hot spots, or areas of high PCB concentration, are located at Fort Edward. Even though the US Environmental Protection Agency (EPA) put Fort Edward on its **Superfund** priority list in 1983, the PCBs remain in the Hudson.

There is a great deal of controversy between environmentalists and other concerned people regarding the best way to clean up the river. Environmentalists believe the PCB contaminated soil should be sucked off the river bottom and put into landfills. Local residents do not want these landfills in their communities. Some scientists even worry that if the PCBs are moved, the contamination will spread downriver.

Although a final decision has yet to be reached, some progress has been made. In addition to banning PCBs and other deadly toxins, legislation now exists to stop the indiscriminate dumping of toxic waste. In 1989, for instance, New York State passed a Hazardous Waste Reduction Act that established legal guidelines for the elimination and reduction of dangerous chemical refuse.

# Canals Connect the River to Farmers

Leaving Fort Edward, we wind our way to Waterford, another example of a Hudson River/Champlain Canal community that thrived in the nineteenth century. Its commercial success centered on its proximity to both the Erie Canal and the Mohawk River. Completed in 1825, the Erie Canal used the Hudson to

*The Hudson Valley orchards are an important source of income for upstate New York farmers.*

link New York City with Buffalo, New York. Flowing into the Hudson from the west, the canal opened the Hudson Valley to the agricultural and commercial wealth developing beyond the Great Lakes.

It was easier to raise wheat in the fertile Midwest than in upstate New York. So, after the Erie Canal opened, wheat farmers moved west. They used the Great Lakes and the

Canal to ship their produce back to New York City and towns along the Hudson. The farmers who remained in upstate New York gave up growing wheat to become dairy farmers and fruit growers.

The Mohawk River, which also joins the Hudson from the west, is the river's largest tributary. It, too, was a vital artery in the industrial growth of the region. The river was named for the Mohawk Indians who lived along its banks for approximately two hundred years before the Dutch began settling the area in 1614.

Once past the Mohawk, we come to the last dam and lock on the harnessed Hudson. With the city of Troy in sight, we head for yet another Hudson, a Hudson that drops only 2 feet (6 m) between here and the ocean, a Hudson that smells of the sea.

*An aerial view of Troy, next to the Hudson River*

# Chapter Four

# The Tidal Hudson

At Troy, the upper river ends and the lower river begins. There are no longer any rapids to maneuver, falls to harness, or dams to contain. There is, however, the strong current of Muhheakantuck, the tidal river that flows both ways. As we learned earlier, the current of the lower Hudson flows in both directions because it is an estuary controlled by ocean tides. Near Troy, the river's low tide drops the water level 4.5 feet (1.4 m) when the tide goes out.

31

## Ocean Tides Affect the Hudson

Ocean tides occur because of gravitational pulls on the earth. Because the moon is closer, its pull is stronger than the sun's. The gravitational force causes the oceans that are facing the moon to bulge out. This bulge creates high tides. When the earth turns on its axis and the oceans move away from the moon, the gravitational pull on them decreases. As a result, the bulge lessens, the water flows back into the sea, and the tide is low. Because the Hudson estuary is on the Atlantic coast, it has two high tides and two low tides approximately every twenty-four hours.

As strong as these tides are, they do not carry the Atlantic's salt this far north. Here, at Troy, the river is still fresh water. Exactly how far north the Hudson's salt line travels depends on each year's spring rain runoff. Generally, the river is salt water up to Newburgh, which is approximately 60 miles (96.5 km) north of New York City. From Newburgh to Poughkeepsie, an additional 15 miles (24 km), the river's water is brackish, which means that it is a mixture of both fresh and salt water.

# River Cities

Troy, founded by Dutch settlers in 1646, played a major role in the country's development. Up through the nineteenth century, the city, which is the gateway between the Hudson's two halves, prospered. Along with Albany, which is just south on the river's west bank, Troy linked the estuary with the expanding canal system on the upper river. Its railroad connected it to the Adirondacks, and its ironworks processed tons of iron ore. The city also boasted that it was the detachable shirt-collar capital of the east.

In 1860, Troy had over fifty thousand residents. Today, that number is almost the same. Because factories moved away from the city, it has lost much of its industrial life. Nevertheless, as is so often the case with river communities, Troy is working to redefine itself for the new century.

Unlike Troy, Albany, with a population of 104,828, continues to expand, spreading out and around the banks of the Hudson. The state capital of New York since 1797, the city is also an active maritime center. As a port of entry for the United States, it processes cargo from all over the world.

*Albany is an important port for shipping.*

## Rip Van Winkle Lies Here on the Hudson

Rip Van Winkle is the main character in a story by Washington Irving, who set many of his stories near the Hudson. First published in 1819, the tale tells of a lazy villager who fell asleep in the Catskill Mountains before the Revolutionary War and woke up twenty years later. Irving once said that he thanked God he "was born on the banks of the Hudson." Still popular today, his stories have added much to the legendary lore of the river.

Leaving Albany's modern skyline behind, the scenery changes when the Hudson winds past the east-bank town of Hudson. The dark purple of the Catskill Mountains rises up on the western horizon and creates spectacular sunsets for this small river community. Between 1770 and 1830, Hudson was a major whaling port that rivaled some of the ports on the Atlantic coast. Today, condominium complexes have taken the place of the tall-masted ships that once hugged the shoreline.

Once past Hudson, the river flows under the Rip Van Winkle Bridge. The eighth bridge since Troy, it is one of fourteen bridges that span the estuary. This one, however, has particular significance because of its name.

Passing by the old town of Saugerties, we are reminded again of the industrial Hudson of the nineteenth century. This now-forgotten town was once famous for its brickyards, paper mills, steamboat landings, and icehouses. The river's first lighthouse is still here. Built in 1838, it was one of many lighthouses that extended from the Hudson's mouth to Troy.

Kingston, which has wide public beaches that look out over the river, is the next major community on the Hudson. About 90 miles (145 km) from New York City, it is a distribution cen-

*A sailboat sails past a marina near Kingston on the Hudson River.*

35

ter for fruits and dairy products produced on surrounding farms. Originally settled by the Dutch, Kingston was the first capital of New York. In the early 1800s, Kingston was known for its steamboat-building industry.

# Steamboats Change River Travel

When Robert Fulton launched the first commercially successful steamboat on August 17, 1807, he revolutionized river travel on the Hudson. Until that time, Hudson River sloops had ruled the river. Designed by the Dutch, the single-masted sailing boats maneuvered well in the Hudson's shallow water. However, they were hindered by the tides. Sloops could not take a load of European goods to Albany or transport Adirondack lumber to New York City unless the winds and the current were favorable.

Fulton's *North River*, which was later renamed the *Clermont*, had no problem with tides. The 130-foot (40-m) long vessel had a steam-powered engine that drove two 15-foot (4.6-m)

*This illustration shows a steamboat going upriver on the Hudson.*

paddle wheels through the water. The boat could make the trip from New York City to Albany in an unheard of thirty-six hours.

After Kingston, the Hudson flows past Hyde Park, the home of President Franklin Delano Roosevelt. Now a museum, the house is hidden from the river by a high bluff. However, if you stand on the porch and look through the trees in the distance, sometimes you can see the massive smokestack of a cargo ship on its way to or from Albany.

*Hyde Park, located on the Hudson, was the home of President Franklin Delano Roosevelt.*

*The **Clearwater** sloop teaches kids to sail on the Hudson.*

# Chapter Five

# The Timeless Hudson

Coming into Poughkeepsie, we enter a stretch of the Hudson where the past and present exist side by side. In the early 1800s, Poughkeepsie, like Hudson to the north, was a major whaling port. Today, this east bank community of thirty thousand is home to a major branch of the IBM computer company. However, tied to a dock we find a reproduction of a Hudson River sloop, a boat that takes us back to a far less technological time.

The sloop looks somewhat lost among

the motor boats and high-rise buildings of the late 1990s, but this 106-foot (32-m) wooden beauty is anything but lost. It is the *Clearwater.*

In 1969, the folk singer and political activist Pete Seeger and other concerned citizens built the *Clearwater* to remind people of "the way it was on the river a hundred years ago." Since the sloop's launch, thousands of school children have worked on it by raising sails, tying knots, charting courses, and learning about the Hudson's ecology.

# Saving Storm King Mountain

Beyond Poughkeepsie, we pass under the Newburgh-Beacon Bridge and enter the Hudson Highlands where Storm King Mountain rises up from the river's west bank. In the 1960s, Storm King was the center of a heated legal debate because Consolidated Edison, New York City's electrical company, wanted to build a large, water-cooled plant into the mountain.

## Hudson Highlands

Storm King and Breakneck Mountain, on the Hudson's east bank, form the northern gateway to the Hudson Highlands. Rising as high as 1,400 feet (427 m), the "endless hills," as the Delaware Indians called the Highlands, stretch for 25 miles (40 km) between the towns of Newburgh and Peekskill.

The strong currents and high winds that funnel through this break in the Appalachian Mountain Range made this section of the Hudson particularly dangerous for early explorers. The Dutch, in fact, named treacherous parts of the Highlands "World's End" and the "Devil's Horse Race."

Conservationists and environmentalists opposed the plan. They said the structure would destroy the natural beauty of the mountain. It took twenty years for the courts to decide, but eventually Storm King was saved.

*You can see why the Hudson highlands are called the "endless hills."*

## Artists Are Inspired by the Hudson

Beginning in the 1820s, the Hudson Highlands inspired the Hudson River School of Painting. Romantic painters, such as Thomas Cole, Frederick Church, and Asher Durand, thought that natural beauty was a gift from God, and they attempted

*Frederick Edwin Church's oil painting of the Hudson in 1850*

to capture this beauty on their canvasses. Many artists also realized that economic growth was introducing civilization to the wilderness. These painters added farms, villages, factories, sailing ships, and steamboats to their landscapes.

Nineteenth century paintings of the Hudson often included views of West Point. Built on a bluff at the southern end of the Highlands, West Point was constructed during the American Revolution to stop British ships from controlling the lower river. Today, the impressive stone buildings of "The Point" house the United States Military Academy.

## The Great Chain

In 1778, the American Army forged a huge iron-linked chain across the Hudson. Called the Great Chain, each link was 2 feet (6 m) long and weighed between 140 and 180 pounds (63 and 82 kg). One end of the chain was anchored to the shore below West Point. The rest was attached to rafts and floated over to Constitution Island, near the Hudson's east bank. The chain was built to stop British ships from sailing upriver. But since no enemy ships ever went that far north, its effectiveness was never tested.

# Toxic Waste in Foundry Cove

Across the Hudson from West Point is the quaint village of Cold Spring. A commuter town for New York City, Cold Spring also has Foundry Cove, the river's second Superfund site. Unlike Fort Edward, which is known for PCBs, Foundry Cove has the dubious distinction of having the world's highest level of cadmium contamination. Cadmium is a heavy-metal waste product created in the production of batteries. It causes kidney damage and possible cancer in humans.

*A worker in protective garb and mask shovels dredged soil that was contaminated with cadmium. The soil will be processed before it is trucked away.*

Built in 1817, the foundry originally made weapons for the army. However, between 1953 and 1979, a battery factory operated at the site and unfortunately poisoned the area with this deadly toxin.

Currently, there is a debate about the best way to clean up this section of the Hudson. Recent plans call for dredging the cadmium-polluted sediment out of the cove, but leaving alone the marsh areas that have less contamination. Clean up of the factory and surrounding land was completed at the end of 1995.

# Continuing Down the River

Passing under Bear Mountain Bridge, built in 1924 as the river's first bridge for automobiles, we come to Dunderberg Mountain. Legend says that the pirate Captain William Kidd buried his treasure here. If true, it has yet to be found.

Then, 26 miles (42 km) south of Peekskill, smokestacks from the Hudson's nuclear power plant at Indian Point rise over the river. This facility produces electricity for the Hudson Valley and New York City.

At Haverstraw Bay, which is 3 miles (5 km) across, we come to the widest part of the Hudson. Despite its width, tidal currents built up sediment so that in some places the bay is only 26 feet (8 m) deep. To accommodate large ships, this sediment is continually dredged out, creating a channel 32 feet (8 m) deep and 600 feet (183 m) wide.

Once out of Haverstraw Bay, we travel to Croton, where we can take a final look back at the timeless Hudson. Down on the river, a replica of Henry Hudson's *Half Moon* is docked at Senasqua Park. Inland, the post-Revolutionary War estate of

the Van Cortlandt family is a living museum where the present becomes the past.

*A replica of Hudson's Half Moon*

At the Croton River, which feeds into the Hudson from the northeast, we return again to the present. In earlier centuries this tributary served the villages and farms surrounding it. Now blocked by dams and huge reservoirs, it is part of the vast Croton Reservoir System that serves New York City. As we pass under the Tappan Zee Bridge at Tarrytown, we see the high towers of that remarkable metropolis hovering on the horizon.

*A view of Piermont Marsh over the lower Hudson*

# Chapter Six

# The Wetlands Meet the Urban Hudson

Below Tarrytown, we are so close to metropolitan New York that commuter trains whiz up and down the Hudson's east bank with clocklike regularity. As frantic as the pace is, when we go into Piermont Marsh just north of New Jersey on the river's west bank, we enter another Hudson. Here, alongside the speeding trains, cars, and steel bridges of

## Wetlands Preserve Nature

Of all the wetlands on the estuary, the Stockport flats, north of Hudson, are the most diverse. This 1,543-acre (624-ha) preserve has 5 miles (8 km) of shoreline that includes freshwater flats, tidal marshes, and swamps. The sandbars and mudflats of the flats form habitats for submerged river plants. The thick reeds of Stockport's marshes protect the Hudson's birds. Finally, the tidal swamps provide a safe haven for the river's fish that **spawn** and spend their early lives in this environment.

urban life is the peaceful natural world of a river wetland. Piermont Marsh is one of twelve **wetlands** on the estuary. Each of these areas is vital to the ecological balance of the river. A variety of birds, animals, and fish depend on the marsh for survival. At Piermont, migratory birds and wintering waterfowl find refuge along the marsh's 2 miles (3 km) of brackish shoreline.

# Pollution Destroys the Wetlands

Unfortunately, pollution threatens all of Hudson's wildlife. Lethal levels of PCBs have been found in the great horned owl, and some animals, such as the mink and river otter, are rarely seen anymore. Toxic contamination has diminished their numbers.

In the 1970s, PCB contamination also destroyed the fishing industry on the Hudson. Today, shad and sturgeon are sold commercially because their PCB levels are below the federal limit, and these fish spend most of their adult life in the ocean.

Nevertheless, in 1994 the New York State Department of Health recommended that women of childbearing age and children under fifteen not eat any fish taken from the estuary.

Luckily, federal and state laws now exist to clean up rivers like the Hudson. The Clean Water Act of 1972 states, in part, that it will "restore and maintain the chemical, physical, and biological integrity of the Nation's waters." The Act also says that wetlands cannot be filled in or dredged if doing so means there will be a "loss of fish and wildlife habitat." Other laws deal specifically with industrial pollution.

## John Cronin, Riverkeeper

For the Hudson to improve, however, it will take more than laws. Public commitment is also necessary. One individual who is committed to the Hudson is John Cronin. An environmentalist, Cronin was hired by the Hudson River Fisherman's Association in 1983 to be the Hudson's riverkeeper. As riverkeeper, Cronin spends much of his time on the river looking for pollution violations. Cronin believes that if people see the Hudson as "a living river from Lake Tear to the sea," they will join together to "respect and care for it."

*Pollution threatens the existence of even the great horned owl.*

*A fisherman catches spring sturgeon on the Hudson. Fishing is an important pastime and occupation.*

# New York, New York

Slipping past the Palisades and under the George Washington Bridge that connects New York to New Jersey, we momentarily forget the river. The skyscrapers rising over Manhattan Island awe us. With an area of only 31 square miles (80 square kilometers), Manhattan is the smallest of New York City's five boroughs. Yet it is the commercial and banking center of the country, if not the world.

"The Big Apple," as New York City is sometimes called, became the metropolis it is today because of its location at the mouth of the Hudson. The river's protected harbor and direct passage to Albany made the city the clearinghouse for all the commerce that spread so rapidly after the Champlain and Erie Canals were built.

With economic growth came an influx of people. In the nineteenth century, steamers docked at the Hudson piers before the new immigrants they carried were taken to the processing station at Ellis Island. During World War II, the wharves were used for military transports that shipped over a million soldiers to the battlefields of Europe. And throughout most of the twentieth century, the piers were docks for elegant ocean liners that had farewell parties famous for their streamers and champagne.

## The Palisades

The Palisades are a series of 500-foot (152-m) volcanic cliffs that stretch along the Hudson's west bank from below Piermont Marsh to Jersey City, New Jersey. Formed from **magma** that moved up through faults in the earth's crust, the Palisades are 1,000 feet (305 m) thick in some places.

Aboriginal people called them *Wehawken Awk,* which means, "rocks that look like trees." So much rock was taken out in the nineteenth century for building material that New York and New Jersey created an interstate park to save the Palisades from further destruction.

*The George Washington Bridge is 3,500 feet long (1,066 meters) and spans the Hudson River, connecting New Jersey and New York.*

*The midtown Manhattan skyline reminds us how a city's growth depends on a water source.*

Today, after a period of disrepair, the river's Manhattan waterfront is coming back. The aircraft carrier, *USS Enterprise*, now a naval museum, is docked on a reconstructed wharf. Cruise liners use other piers. One wharf is a vast sports complex where enthusiasts climb walls, practice golf, or ice-skate.

Beyond Manhattan, the Hudson flows past the Statue of Liberty and Ellis Island. Here in upper New York Bay, the Hudson meets the East River that flows in from the east. In the distance, the Verrazano-Narrows Bridge spans the Narrows.

The Verrazano-Narrows Bridge is so long—4,260 feet (1,298 m)—that its suspension towers are 1⅝ inches farther apart at the top than they are at their bases. The difference compensates for the curvature of the earth.

*The Verrazano-Narrows Bridge is named after Giovanni da Verrazano, who sailed into New York Bay in the sixteenth century.*

# Leaving the River

We are now at the end of our trip down the Hudson. As the nineteenth-century historian Benson J. Lossing said after his voyage 130 years ago, "We have had a pleasant and memorable journey from the wilderness. We have seen every phase of material progress, from nature in her wildest form to civilization in its highest development."

We have traveled the river from its beginnings on Mount Marcy to its end in New York Bay. We have seen the quiet world of nature and the industrial world of humankind. So, as we watch the gray-green, blue-green water of the Hudson rush out to meet the Atlantic Ocean, we now understand how remarkable this rich river of opposites truly is.

# Glossary

**Bering Land Bridge**—the large landmass that formed approximately twenty thousand years ago when there was a continual drop in sea level. The "bridge" allowed the first migration of humans from northeast Asia into northwestern North America.

**canal**—an artificial waterway used for transportation or irrigation

**conservationist**—a person who works to protect natural resources from waste or loss

**continental shelf**—part of the continent, the continental shelf is a submerged platform that dips gradually toward the ocean

**ecology**—the study of relationships between animals and their environments

**environmentalist**—a person who works to solve such environmental problems as air, water, and soil pollution

**estuary**—sunken river beds where fresh river water mixes with sea water from the ocean

**forge**—a furnace to heat and melt metal so that it can be hammered into a shape

**lock**—a part of a canal that serves as a water elevator to move ships up and down to the next section of the canal

**magma**—molten rock material within the earth from which igneous rock results from cooling

**spawn**—reproduce

**Superfund**—name for the Comprehensive Environmental Response, Compensation, and Liability Act passed by Congress in 1980; administered by the US Environmental Protection Agency, Superfund oversees the monetary funding for cleanups of toxic-waste sites

**surveyor**—a person who studies and maps out a particular area of land

**toxicity**—poisonous levels

**watershed**—an area of land that drains water into a particular river or river system

**wetlands**—areas of land where plants and animals live in shallow water

# To Find Out More

## Books

Durrant, Lynda. *Echo Hawk*. New York: Dial, 1996.

Heinrichs, Ann. *New York* (America the Beautiful Series). Danbury, Connecticut: Grolier Publishing, 1999.

Lourie, Peter. *Hudson River—An Adventure from the Mountains to the Sea*. Honesdale, Pennsylvania: Caroline House, 1992.

Sterman, Betsy. *Saratoga Secret*. New York: Dial, 1998.

Tagliaferro, Linda. *Destination New York, Port Series of North America*. Minneapolis, Minnesota: Lerner, 1998.

Thompson, Kathleen. *New York* (Portrait of America Series). Austin, Texas: Raintree Steck-Vaughn, 1996.

# Organizations and Online Sites

Hudson River Sloop Clearwater, Inc.
112 Market St.
Poughkeepsie, NY 12601
*http://www.clearwater.org*
This is an informative Internet site filled with photos, videos, and music. The site gives a history of the Hudson River sloop, *Clearwater*, tells about the Clearwater organization, and also explains how concerned citizens can get involved to save the river.

The Hudson River Fisherman's Association
New Jersey Chapter
P.O. Box 421
Cresskill, NJ 07676
*http://www.hrfanj.org*
This organization is a good online source for information on lower Hudson River conditions. It offers environmental news, political contacts, and fishing reports.

Electric Times Union Newspaper
Albany, New York
*www.timesunion.com*
This newspaper online site has a particularly good article about the river entitled "The Hudson River Chronicles." This site, which is part of the Electric Times Union from Albany, New York, gives information about the river from the Adirondacks to New York City. It also has a section called "River Voices," which is an audio file of people talking about their experiences on the Hudson.

The Adirondack Museum
P.O. Box 99
Blue Mountain Lake, NY 12812-0099
*http://www.adkmuseum.org.*
You should certainly visit this museum in person if you can. However, if you live across the country, this online site is a terrific alternative for information about the history of the Adirondacks, news about museum collections, listings of upcoming events in the mountains, and much more. The museum is dedicated to the history, culture, and appreciation of the Adirondacks.

# A Note on Sources

Whenever I do research, I start at the library. The library, with its vast collection of books, encyclopedias, magazines, and Internet sources, is a terrific reservoir of knowledge. Usually, I begin by looking up my subject in an encyclopedia. The information in the encyclopedia gives me a general overview that I can fill out in greater detail by then finding information in books and magazines. I use Internet sources to add any extra details I might want. If I find new information on the Internet, I always confirm it with additional research.

Sometimes, however, I start with books. For instance, when I began my work on the Hudson, I read Peter Lourie's book, *A River of Mountains, A Canoe Journey Down the Hudson*. Lourie's account of his trip down the river helped me visualize the entire length of the Hudson. I also read Nina H. Webb's *Verplanck Colvin, Footsteps Through the Adirondacks*. Webb's biography of the famous New York State surveyor helped me understand the important connections between the Hudson River and the Adirondack State Park.

Museums are also rich gold mines of information. For this book, I spent two days at the Adirondack Museum in Blue Mountain Lake, New York. The museum not only has a terrific library that introduced me to the writings of Benson Lossing, but it also has detailed displays and reconstructed houses that traced the history of the area.

Because I am lucky enough to live near the Hudson, I also used my own experience of the river when writing this book. I have picnicked on the Adirondack Hudson and crossed the river at the George Washington Bridge more times than I can count.

— *Melissa Whitcraft*

# Index

Numbers in *italics* indicate illustrations.

# About the Author

Melissa Whitcraft lives in Montclair, New Jersey with her husband, their two sons, and their dog. She has a Masters in Art in Theatre. In addition to plays and poetry, she has written both fiction and nonfiction for children. She has published *Tales From One Street Over*, a chapter book for early elementary-grade readers. Her biography, *Francis Scott Key, a Gentleman of Maryland*, was published as a Franklin Watts First Book. Ms. Whitcraft has also written another river book about the Tigris and Euphrates Rivers for the Watts Library series. Whenever possible, Ms. Whitcraft travels on rivers and is grateful she lives so near the Hudson.